CONTENTS

INTRODUCTION

Paul Pogba helped France to a 2018 World Cup victory. Pogba scored one of his team's goals during its 4–2 final win over Croatia.

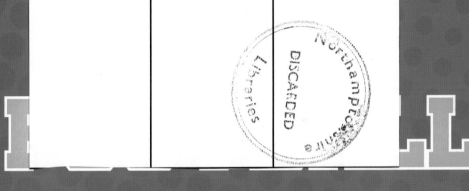

A Guide for Players and Fans

HEATHER WILLIAMS

raintree

Raintree is an imprint of Capstone Global Library Limited, a company incorporated in England and Wales having its registered office at 264 Banbury Road, Oxford, OX2 7DY – Registered company number: 6695582

www.raintree.co.uk
myorders@raintree.co.uk

Edited by Lauren Dupuis-Perez
Designed by Sara Radka
Original illustrations © Capstone Global Library Limited 2020
Picture research by Eric Gohl
Production by Laura Manthe
Originated by Capstone Global Library Ltd
Printed and bound in India

978 1 4747 8876 2 (hardback)
978 1 4747 8878 6 (paperback)

British Library Cataloguing in Publication Data
A full catalogue record for this book is available from the British Library.

Acknowledgements
We would like to thank the following for permission to reproduce photographs: Getty Images: Buda Mendes, cover (foreground), Catherine Ivill, 17, Dan Mullan, 23, Dean Mouhtaropoulos, 28 (bottom), EyeEm/Zhihua Hu, 11 (front), fstop123, 29, Ian Walton, 19, Jasper Juinen, 22, Laurence Griffiths, 24, Matthias Hangst, 4, Michael Reaves, 20, SerrNovik, 28 (top), monkeybusinessimages, cover (background), Steve Debenport, 27, The Good Brigade, 14; Pixabay: intographics, background; Shutterstock: Eugene Onischenko, 10-11, Goran Bogicevic, 12 (bottom), imstock, 12 (top), OSTILL is Franck Camhi, 18, Who is Danny, 8-9; Wikimedia: State Library of South Australia, 7, Unknown, 9, www.twylah.com, 6

Every effort has been made to contact copyright holders of material reproduced in this book. Any omissions will be rectified in subsequent printings if notice is given to the publisher.

Football teams from countries around the world compete in the World Cup every four years. The international football **tournament** attracts huge crowds of devoted fans. The World Cup is so popular that one country built a brand new city for it! Since 2005, the city of Lusail in Qatar has grown from a tiny village to a huge city with skyscrapers and shopping centres. Nine new stadiums are being built for the 2022 World Cup.

More than a billion people watched the 2018 World Cup Final. Famous players such as Antoine Griezmann and Luca Modric played in the match. Superstars such as Lionel Messi from Argentina and Neymar from Brazil keep football in the spotlight. But away from the fame, approximately 3.35 million children in the UK regularly play football. People of all ages love watching and playing football.

tournament contest in which the winner is the one who wins the most games

People have been playing some form of football for many centuries. The sport as we now know it, however, started in England in the 1800s. A group of players decided football needed clearer rules. They did not like the way some people played. The game often got rough and sometimes included shin-kicking, tripping and even biting. Also, some players often picked up the ball and ran with it. The group decided on rules and founded the Football Association (FA) in 1863. The FA was the first professional football **league** in the world.

Harry Thickett played for Sheffield United in the late 1800s and early 1900s.

league group of teams that play against each other

Teams started forming all over the UK. British sailors and traders taught the game to people in countries they visited. Football became popular across Europe and South America. By 1904, there were many football teams around the world. The Fédération Internationale de Football Association

Historians have called the 1920s the "Golden Age of Sport". Football gained popularity, and new teams were formed around the world. This photo is of an Australian team.

(FIFA) was founded to make sure that all the teams follow the rules. FIFA also plans tournaments such as the World Cup.

Football was one of the first sports to build large stadiums to host games. The Centenario, in Uruguay, was built to host the first World Cup in 1930.

Many countries have professional football leagues. The English Premier League is the most popular league in the world. There are 20 teams in the league and they play each other twice every season.

Many countries have **national teams** for men and women. The England women's team has become very popular with fans in recent years. The team has competed at the Women's World Cup 5 times since 1995. Their best result was when they finished third in 2015.

The US women's national team is the most successful women's team of all time. They have won four World Cups and four Olympic gold medals.

At the 1999 FIFA Women's World Cup, about 90,000 people came to watch the them play China. It was a record high for women's football.

FACT

In the original rules of football, written in 1863, there was no height requirement for the goal. A player could score a goal as long as the ball passed between two goal posts. This is similar to a conversion in rugby.

national team team chosen to represent the country where players live

1863

1904

1930

1991

2015

After hundreds of years of a rough and rowdy form of the game, the Football Association is established to bring order to football.

Fédération Internationale de Football Association is founded to oversee the growth of football around the world.

The first World Cup for men's football is played. More than 68,000 people pack in to the stadium to watch the final.

The US women's team wins the first ever Women's World Cup. Team captain Michelle Akers scores both of the US's goals to beat Norway 2–1 in the final.

The Women's FA Cup Final is played at Wembley Stadium for the first time. The match is attended by over 30,000 fans.

The first World Cup

The first World Cup took place in 1930. It was held in Uruguay in South America. The team from Uruguay had won the gold medal at the 1928 Olympics. Uruguay was building football stadiums and had lots of room for the World Cup. Teams came from Europe, North America and South America. Uruguay won the final match against Argentina. The result was 4–2.

Not much equipment was needed to play the very first football matches. Players only had two pieces of equipment: a goal and a ball. Early balls were made from animal skins. Some were pigs' bladders filled with air! The first rubber ball that could be filled with air was made in 1862. The FA made the first official football design. Today, players need a few more items. Special socks and boots, and some safety equipment, are required.

1

2

3

4

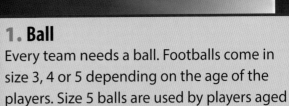

1. Ball
Every team needs a ball. Footballs come in size 3, 4 or 5 depending on the age of the players. Size 5 balls are used by players aged 12 years and older.

2. Socks
Football socks help protect lower legs and keep shin guards in place. All players on a team have to wear matching socks.

3. Shin pads
Hard plastic shields protect shins and ankles from kicks. No player is allowed to step on the pitch without them.

4. Boots
Football boots have rubber or metal studs on the bottom. They help players run on grass without slipping.

5. Goal
Every pitch has two goals. The size depends on the age of the players, but standard goals are 2.4 metres (8 feet) high and 7.3 metres (8 yards) wide. Goals are usually made of a metal frame and a cloth net.

5

Equipment for the players

Shin pads protect parts of the leg that are not protected by muscle or tissue.

A few safety items are required for football. Shin pads are the number-one required safety items for players. They are made of hard plastic. Shin pads fit over the lower legs. They keep players' shins and ankles safe from hard kicks. Players usually attach shin pads to their legs with soft straps. Special football socks hold them in place. Players of all ages and levels have to wear shin pads. All players must wear football boots with studs on the bottom. They help players run on grass.

FACT

The first rubber football was invented in 1855 by Charles Goodyear. It was brown. The popular black-and-white panelled ball did not hit pitches until the 1960s.

12

Sometimes footballers choose to wear protective headgear. Padded helmets that look like wide headbands protect the skull. Footballers can injure their brain when they use their heads to pass the ball. This is called heading. They can also bump heads with another player. This can cause a **concussion**. Headgear can help to prevent concussions. The most famous example of this is Petr Cech who began wearing protective headgear after he suffered an injury.

The goalkeeper on a team has some extra items. He or she wears special gloves to grip the ball. They can also wear padded shorts and shirts. Goalkeepers also wear different coloured tops. This way the teams and officials can tell the goalkeepers apart from other players.

Tsu chu (or cuju)

One of the earliest forms of football was called *tsu' chu* or *cuju*. It was played in China more than 2,000 years ago. The game was part of the training programme for Chinese soldiers. *Tsu* means "kicking with feet" and *chu* means "ball". Players had to kick a ball through a small hole in a net 9 metres (30 feet) above the pitch. Today's players are lucky the net is on the ground!

concussion injury to the brain caused by a hard blow to the head

In youth football, team sizes range from no more than 4 players to no more than 11 players per team, depending on the age of the players.

There were no rules in the very first football matches. Today there are 17 basic rules of football. Some rules keep players safe; others make sure players everywhere understand how the game works. There are also rules about how many players can be on the pitch.

A team has 11 players including the goalkeeper. Youth teams have fewer players and play on smaller pitches. The goalkeeper is the only player who can pick up the ball on the pitch. Goalkeepers try to stop the ball from going into the goal. Teams also have defenders who play in front of the goal. Defenders try to keep the ball away from their own goal. Midfielders play between the defenders and forwards. They help to defend, but they often score goals too. Forwards (also called strikers) are the players who score most of the goals. They play closest to the other team's goal.

Every football pitch has touch lines, goal lines and **penalty** areas painted on the ground. If a ball goes over a touch line, a player throws it back into the match. This is called a throw-in. If a player kicks the ball off the pitch at his or her own goal line, the other team gets a corner kick. If a player kicks the ball across the other team's goal line, the other team gets a goal kick.

Football matches are usually 90 minutes long. The match is split into two 45-minute halves with a half-time break in between. Youth matches usually have 20- to 35-minute halves. The length of time depends on the age group. In most matches, a **draw** is okay. In the final stages of tournaments, if the match is a draw, extra time is added. If it's still a draw after extra time, a penalty shootout takes place. Players get to shoot the ball from a spot 11 metres (12 yards) from the goal.

penalty punishment for breaking the rules
draw when a game ends with both sides having the same score

If a player from one team kicks a ball off the pitch, a player from the other team is awarded a throw-in from the spot the ball left the pitch. A player throws the ball in from outside the pitch boundaries to members of their team. A goal cannot be scored by throwing the ball into the net.

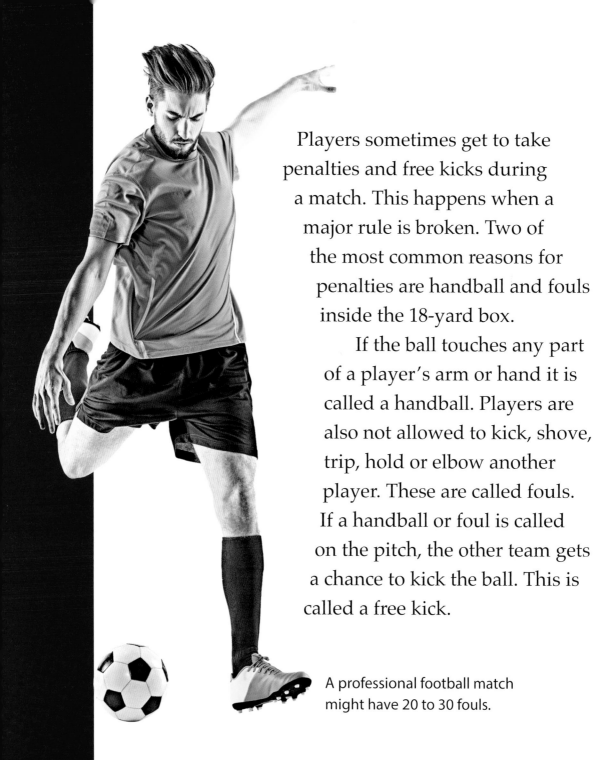

Players sometimes get to take penalties and free kicks during a match. This happens when a major rule is broken. Two of the most common reasons for penalties are handball and fouls inside the 18-yard box.

If the ball touches any part of a player's arm or hand it is called a handball. Players are also not allowed to kick, shove, trip, hold or elbow another player. These are called fouls. If a handball or foul is called on the pitch, the other team gets a chance to kick the ball. This is called a free kick.

A professional football match might have 20 to 30 fouls.

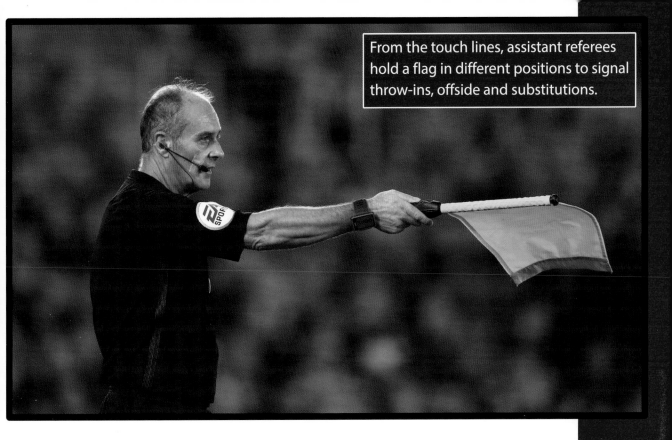

From the touch lines, assistant referees hold a flag in different positions to signal throw-ins, offside and substitutions.

During a football match, a player is not allowed to kick the ball to a teammate who is closer to the goal than the other team's second-to-last player, including the goalkeeper. This is called being offside. Before the offside rule, players could stay in front of the other team's goal and wait for the ball to come to them. This made scoring too easy.

FACT

Referees were not used in football until 1891. Before that, a player from each team enforced rules during matches.

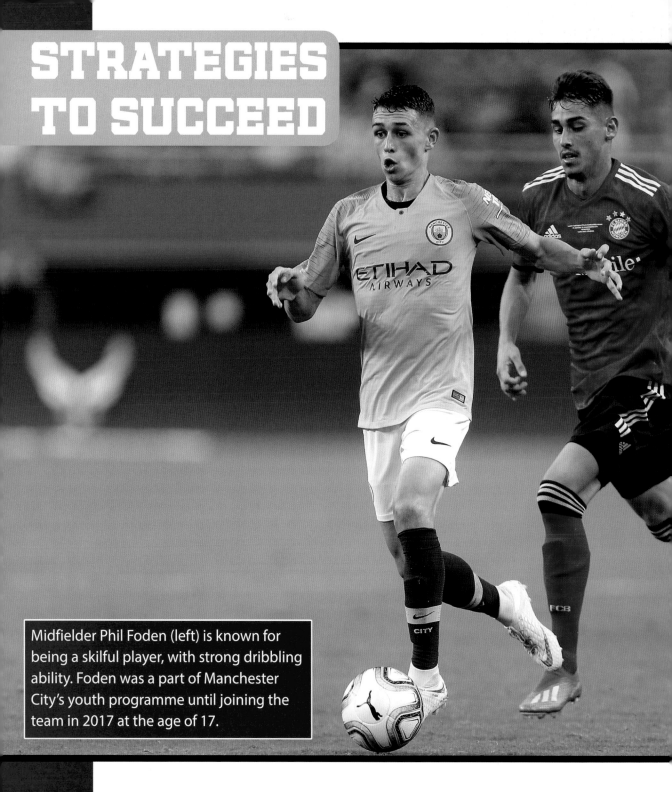

STRATEGIES TO SUCCEED

Midfielder Phil Foden (left) is known for being a skilful player, with strong dribbling ability. Foden was a part of Manchester City's youth programme until joining the team in 2017 at the age of 17.

A football team has two jobs. One is to score goals. The other is to prevent the other team from scoring. When a team is trying to score it is called attacking. When a team is trying to stop the other team from scoring it is called defending.

Trapping and controlling the ball are important for both attacking and defending. Trapping means that a player uses his or her body to stop the ball. Players can use any part of the body except the arms and hands to trap the ball. Once a player traps the ball, it is important to control it. Players can **dribble** or pass the ball. Players can dribble without looking at the ball. A player must be able to look around and find the best teammate to receive a pass. Kicking the ball to a teammate is called passing. Passes can be to nearby teammates or over a longer distance.

dribble move the ball along by kicking it with your feet

A team that has control of the ball is the attacking team. They are moving the ball towards their opponents' goal. The attacking team never stops moving. Players pass and then keep moving so they can be a target for a pass. By moving into open spaces, players can create chances to score.

Sometimes defenders stop the attacking team from passing the ball. The attacking team has to try longer passes when this happens. These long passes can go from one side of the pitch to the other. Passing like this is called switching play. Players can also pass back towards their own goal. The goalkeeper can then kick a long ball to the other end of the pitch. These are different ways to find a new path to the goal.

Forward Cristiano Ronaldo averages nearly one goal per game.

A corner kick has similar rules to a throw-in, except it is awarded when a defending player kicks the ball off the pitch over the goal line. The attacking team is then allowed to kick from a marked area at the corner of the pitch.

The attacking team can also use free kicks and corner kicks to score. These are called set pieces. Teams can set up plays during set pieces. For example, four or five players can line up in front of the goal and be ready to score from their team's corner kick.

During the 2018 FA Cup Final match in 2018, Chelsea forward Eden Hazard was fouled by a Manchester United player. The penalty scored by Hazard led to Chelsea's 1–0 win.

It is fun to score, but teams need a good defence to win a football match. Some teams use man-to-man defence. This means each player marks a player from the other team. Usually a team's midfielders mark the other team's midfielders. Defenders mark the opponent's forwards, and forwards mark the opponent's defenders.

When defending, a player should always try to be closer to their own goal than the attacker. This is an important part of defending in football. It is called being goal side. Strong defenders stay close to the player they are defending. This forces the player to pass the ball. Stealing the ball from a player who is dribbling is called a tackle.

When a defender gets the ball, he or she can pass it to another defender or clear the ball away. Most defenders choose to clear the ball or kick it towards their own midfielders or forwards.

Lionel Messi

Lionel Messi is one of the greatest footballers of all time. With his team, Barcelona, he has won 10 league titles and 4 UEFA Champions League trophies. He has scored more than 600 goals for Barcelona! Messi has also won many awards. In 2014, he was given the award for being the best player at the FIFA World Cup. In 2019, he was awarded his sixth Golden Shoe for the most goals scored in a season.

READY TO PLAY?

Young people who want to play football are in luck! Football is one of the most popular outdoor youth sports in the world. Watching football is a great way to learn the rules and positions. You can watch matches on TV or a live match.

Players new to the game need to practise the basics. Dribbling the ball with your feet and gaining more ball control through practice is important. Local parks with football pitches are a great place to practise running with a football. Playing with friends is another way to improve your football skills.

Running and exercising will help the body get stronger. Footballers run a lot! Drinking lots of water helps the body to work properly. Eating well is important too. Being fit will make playing on a football team much easier.

Football practice can last about an hour. A coach might decide to spend 10 minutes warming up, 20 minutes working on technique and skills, and 30 minutes on matches.

Joining a team

New players can sign up with a local club or community team. These teams have programmes for boys and girls of all ages. You can also join your school team.

Getting the right equipment is important. A salesperson at a sports shop can make sure players get correct sizes. Every player needs his or her own ball, shin pads and boots. Most teams give players a kit to wear for matches. Players will need a few pairs of football socks and shorts.

FACT

Nooit Opgeven Altijd Doorzetten, Aangenaam Door Vermaak En Nuttig Door Ontspanning, Combinatie Breda is the full name of a professional football team in the Netherlands. In English, the name means "Never give up, always persevere, pleasant for its entertainment and useful for its relaxation, Combination Breda". It is one of the longest team names in the world.

Whether you play at the park or as part of a club team, football is a great way to keep fit and have fun!

Beginners should be willing to learn more than one position on the pitch. Knowing how to play defensive and attacking positions helps players to improve. The most important rule is to have fun. Learning a new sport can be hard, but playing on a team is a great way to learn and make new friends.

Glossary

concussion injury to the brain caused by a hard blow to the head

draw when a game ends with both sides having the same score

dribble move the ball along by kicking it with your feet

league group of teams that play against each other

national team team chosen to represent the country where players live

penalty punishment for breaking the rules

tournament contest in which the winner is the one who wins the most games

Find out more

Books

A-Z of the World Cup (World Cup Fever), Michael Hurley (Raintree, 2014)

Football (DK Eyewitness), Hugh Hornby (DK Children, 2018)

Messi: From the Playground to the Pitch (Ultimate Football Heroes), Matt and Tom Oldfield (Dino Books, 2017)

Websites

www.bbc.co.uk/cbbc/shows/match-of-the-day-kickabout

www.dkfindout.com/uk/sports/football

https://grassroots.fifa.com/en/for-kids.html

Index